A+
books

Counting Books

Counting Pets by Twos

by Rebecca Fjelland Davis

Reading Consultant: Gail Saunders-Smith, PhD

Capstone
press

Mankato, Minnesota

A+ Books are published by Capstone Press,
151 Good Counsel Drive, P.O. Box 669, Mankato, Minnesota 56002.
www.capstonepress.com

1 2 3 4 5 6 11 10 09 08 07 06

Library of Congress Cataloging-in-Publication Data
Davis, Rebecca Fjelland.
    Counting pets by twos / by Rebecca Fjelland Davis.
    p. cm.—(A+ books. Counting books)
    Summary: "Simple text and color photos introduce common pets while counting by twos to
twenty"—Provided by publisher.
    Includes bibliographical references and index.
    ISBN-13: 978-0-7368-6375-9 (hardcover)
    ISBN-10: 0-7368-6375-3 (hardcover)
    1. Counting—Juvenile literature. 2. Pets—Juvenile literature. I. Title. II. Series.
QA113.D3777 2007
513.2'11—dc22   2005038065

Credits
Jenny Marks, editor; Ted Williams, designer; Kelly Garvin, photo researcher/photo editor

Photo Credits
Ardea/John Daniels, 8–9
Brand X Pictures, 11, 16 (one goldfish), 17 (two goldfish), 26 (all goldfish),
    27 (all goldfish)
Capstone Press/Karon Dubke, back cover (all hermit crabs, all dog treats), 12,
    13, 14–15, 20, 21 (crickets), 22–23 (dog biscuits), 26 (hamsters, crickets),
    27 (dog biscuits)
Corbis/Ariel Skelley, 3; DK Limited, cover (all goldfish); T. Hemmings/zefa, 25;
    Tim Davis, 18, 19
Digital Vision, 6–7, 10, 28
Getty Images/GK & Vikki Hart, 5
Shutterstock/George Brunton, 21 (chameleon); ijansempoi, 16 (two goldfish),
    17 (one goldfish); Johanna Goodyear, 16 (three goldfish), 17 (one goldfish);
    Luis Castro, 29
Stockbyte, 22 (dog)

Note to Parents, Teachers, and Librarians
Counting Pets by Twos uses color photographs and a nonfiction format to introduce
children to various types of pets while building mastery of basic counting skills. It is
designed to be read aloud to a pre-reader or to be read independently by an early reader.
The images help early readers and listeners understand the text and concepts discussed.
The book encourages further learning by including the following sections: How Many,
Facts about Pets, Glossary, Read More, Internet Sites, and Index. Early readers may need
assistance using these features.

What's more fun than your very own pet? Double the fun with beaks, tails, and scales by counting pets by twos.

2

Two blue parakeets chirp all day. From squawking to talking, parakeets love to make noise.

Four smart dogs sit when they are told. Dogs can learn to sit, shake hands, and roll over.

6

Six bunny ears perk right up.
When bunnies listen, they
stop hopping and sit still.

Eight cat claws are nice and sharp. Cats are born to scratch, so they need a post or pad for play.

10

Ten hamster eyes shine beady and black. Hamsters' eyes look all around, but a hamster can't see far past the end of its nose.

Twelve hermit crabs stroll across the sand. When a hermit crab outgrows its shell, it finds a new one to fit its body.

12

14

Fourteen goldfish dart through the water. Their shiny orange scales sparkle when they swim.

Sixteen hairy tarantula legs look
creepy as they crawl. Tarantulas
use their strong legs to dig
burrows in sand.

16

18

Eighteen crickets make a tasty meal for this chameleon. After crunching a bunch of crickets, chameleons snooze for a while on a warm rock.

20

Twenty biscuits are a treat for any dog. Reward your pup with treats that keep his teeth clean and bright.

We've counted all kinds of pets by twos. Which pet would be the perfect pal for you?

How Many?

Hamsters

Crickets

Goldfish

Dog Biscuits

27

Facts about Pets

Parakeets come in many colors like blue, yellow, green, and white. Parakeets can learn to talk and perch on people's fingers.

If you have a hamster in your room, it may keep you awake at night. Hamsters are nocturnal animals. They sleep during the day and are active at night.

Dogs and cats are the most popular pets in the United States. Golden retrievers and labrador retrievers are the most popular dogs. The most popular cats are calicos.

Goldfish do not have eyelids. They rest at night with their eyes wide open.

Desert blond tarantulas are often kept as pets. These spiders do not spin webs to catch their food. They hunt for their food by chasing it. Crickets are a tasty food for pet tarantulas.

Hermit crabs can't survive in dry places. A small dish of water with a chunk of natural sea sponge in it will keep the air in a pet hermit crab's tank nice and moist.

Glossary

burrow (BUR-oh)—a hole in the ground in which an animal lives

calico (KAL-i-koh)—a kind of cat that has spotted colors

nocturnal (nok-TUR-nuhl)—active at night and resting during the day

perch (PURCH)—to sit or stand on the edge of something

reward (ri-WAWRD)—to give a pet a treat for doing something well; dog owners reward their pets when they do tricks.

scale (SKALE)—one of the small pieces of hard skin that cover the body of a fish or reptile

squawk (SKWAWK)—to make a loud screech

stroll (STROHL)—to walk slowly

Read More

Blackledge, Annabel. *Small Pet Care: How to Look After Your Rabbit, Guinea Pig, or Hamster.* New York: DK Publishing, 2005.

Loves, June. *Dogs.* Pets. Philadelphia: Chelsea Clubhouse, 2004.

Rayner, Matthew. *Cat.* I Am Your Pet. Milwaukee: Gareth Stevens, 2004.

Rustad, Martha E. H. *Snakes.* All about Pets. Mankato, Minn.: Capstone Press, 2002.

Internet Sites

FactHound offers a safe, fun way to find Internet sites related to this book. All of the sites on FactHound have been researched by our staff.

Here's how:

1. Visit *www.facthound.com*

2. Choose your grade level.

3. Type in this book ID **0736863753** for age-appropriate sites. You may also browse subjects by clicking on letters, or by clicking on pictures and words.

4. Click on the **Fetch It** button.

FactHound will fetch the best sites for you!

Index